Lots of things
you want to know about
GLADIATORS
...and some
you don't!

Written and illustrated by
David West

W

FRANKLIN WATTS
LONDON·SYDNEY

First published in the UK in 2014 by Franklin Watts

Franklin Watts
338 Euston Road
London NW1 3BH

Franklin Watts
Level 17/207 Kent Street
Sydney, NSW 2000

Dewey classification: 796.8'0937

A CIP catalogue record for this book is available from the British Library.

ISBN: 978 1 4451 2718 7

Franklin Watts is a division of Hachette Children's Books, an Hachette UK company.
www.hachette.co.uk

LOTS OF THINGS YOU WANT TO KNOW ABOUT GLADIATORS ...AND SOME YOU DON'T!
David West Children's Books, 6 Princeton Court, 55 Felsham Road, London SW15 1AZ

Designed and illustrated by David West

Printed in China

CONTENTS

Most gladiators were slaves or captured enemy soldiers

The mighty Roman army captured many enemy soldiers while fighting for new lands to extend its huge empire. The captives might be sent to work in mines or sold as slaves, or sold for gladiator training.

Some free young men chose to give up their freedom to enlist as gladiators.

Gladiators trained at special schools

A gladiator was a trained fighter. He was owned by a master to whom he swore an oath of loyalty. Gladiator school offered training, regular food and a fighting chance of fame and fortune.

Gladiators could keep their prize money and any gifts they received.

Gladiators fought in arenas called **amphitheatres**

Around 230 of these oval or circular arenas have been found across the **Roman Empire**. The largest of these is the Colosseum in Rome. It had seating for 50,000 spectators.

The contests had two referees

Most gladiator matches had a senior referee and an assistant. The referees were equipped with long wooden staffs. They used these to signal a caution or to separate the gladiators during the match.

Some gladiators wore armour

The heavily-armoured gladiators, called murmillos and secutors, carried a short sword, called a gladius, and a curved, rectangular shield called a scutum. They wore an arm guard, called a manica, metal leg protectors, called ocras, and a helmet.

Some gladiators used a net

A net fighter was called a retiarius. They were armed with a three-pronged spear called a trident. The retiarius was lightly armoured and wore a manica and one or two ocras. The retiarius usually fought against the heavily-armed secutor.

He used the net to entangle his opponent before finishing him off with his trident.

Some gladiators fought on horseback

Gladiators who fought on horseback were called equites. They started on horseback, but after they had thrown their lance, called a hasta, they dismounted. They continued to fight on foot with their short sword.

Others fought from chariots

Gladiators who fought from chariots were called essedariuses. Chariots might have been introduced to the fights by the Roman leader **Julius Caesar**. He was impressed by the chariots the ancient Britons used against his troops when he invaded Britain in 55 BCE.

Some gladiators fought lions

Gladiators called bestiarii fought wild animals such as lions, tigers, bears and elephants in the arena. These mock hunts were held in the morning before the afternoon's main event of gladiatorial duels. Few animals survived, although sometimes bestiarii were killed by animals.

A defeated gladiator raised his finger

To start with, a gladiator fight usually ended with one contestant dying. Later, as more gladiators were needed, a defeated gladiator might be spared. When a gladiator thought he was close to being killed, he raised his finger to stop the fight.

The crowd decided the fate of a defeated gladiator

Once a gladiator had raised his finger the referees would stop the fight. The man paying for the games, called the **editor**, would grant life or death, according to the shouts of the crowd.

A gladiator's favourite prize was a wooden sword

The winner received a branch of a palm tree and an award from the editor. A really good fighter might receive a laurel crown and money. The greatest reward was freedom. This was symbolised by a wooden sword, given by the editor.

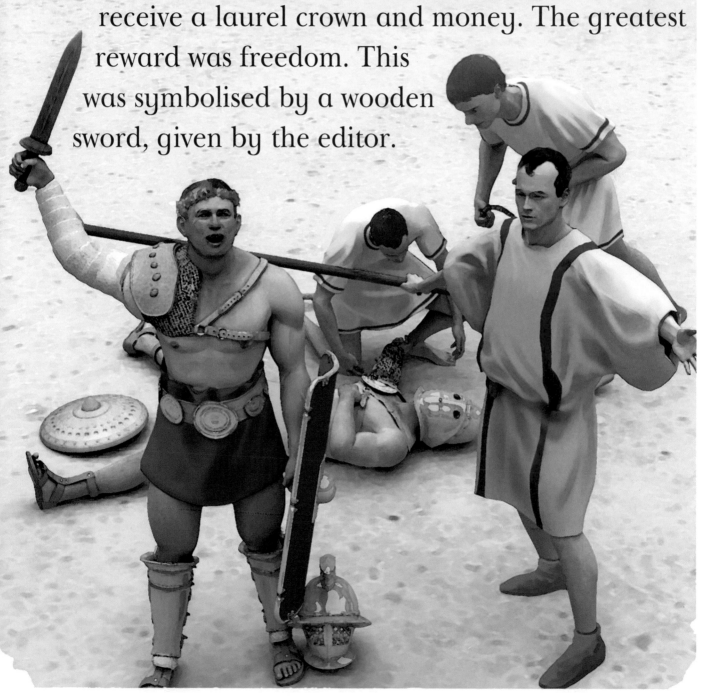

Some gladiator fights ended in a draw

Winning a fight without causing injury was praised. Several gladiators have been recorded as never injuring anyone in their entire careers. Some matches could end in a draw when both gladiators gave up at the same time after a lengthy fight.

Gladiators had fans like modern-day football stars

Although they were slaves, successful gladiators were idolised by the public. Paintings of gladiators were displayed before the fights. If people knew that gladiators were going to be on parade, they would flock to the site and fight for a view. A **senator**'s wife even **eloped** to Egypt with a gladiator called Sergius.

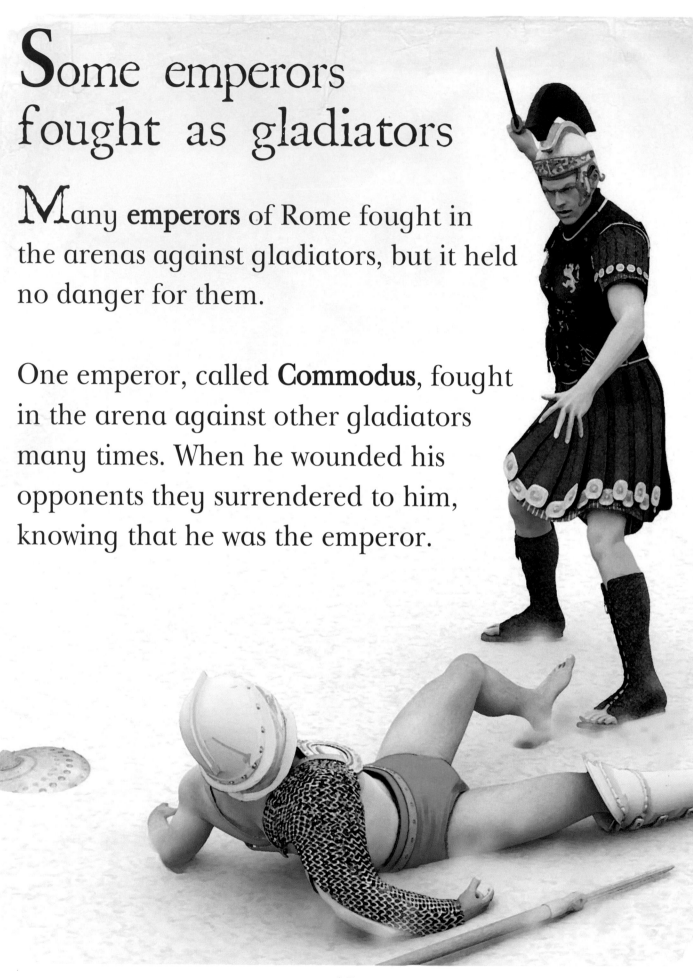

Some emperors fought as gladiators

Many **emperors** of Rome fought in the arenas against gladiators, but it held no danger for them.

One emperor, called **Commodus**, fought in the arena against other gladiators many times. When he wounded his opponents they surrendered to him, knowing that he was the emperor.

Gladiators could become rich and powerful

After keeping all their prize money and gifts, many gladiators bought their freedom and retired in comfort. The emperor **Tiberius** offered several retired gladiators the equivalent of £300,000 each to return to the arena. The general **Mark Antony** promoted gladiators to his personal guard.

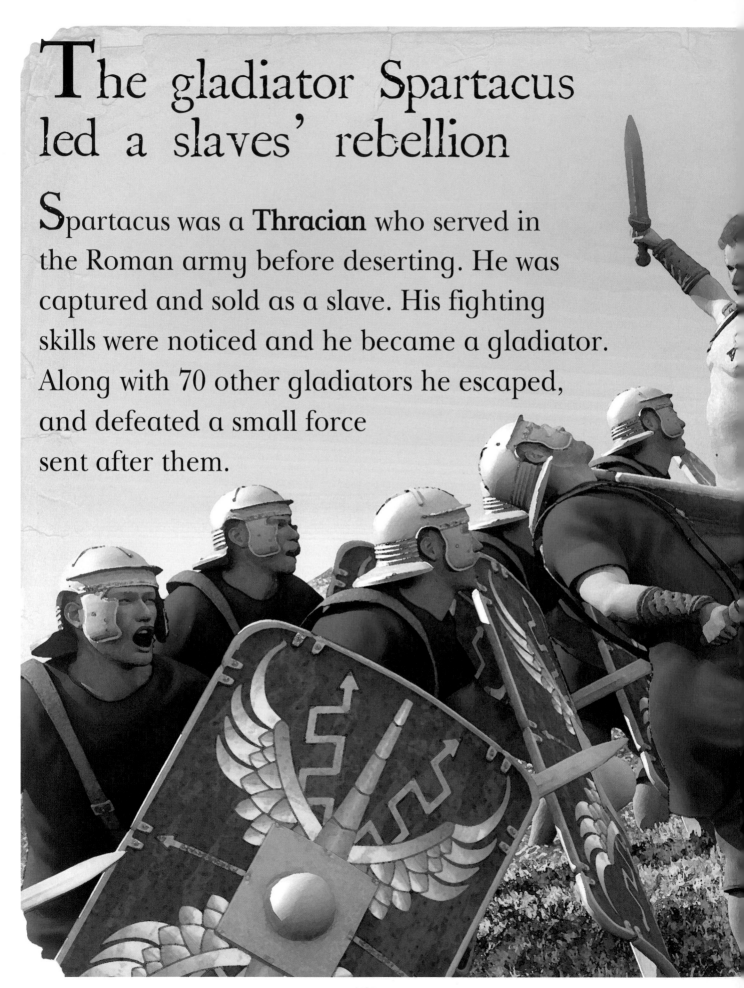

The gladiator Spartacus led a slaves' rebellion

Spartacus was a **Thracian** who served in the Roman army before deserting. He was captured and sold as a slave. His fighting skills were noticed and he became a gladiator. Along with 70 other gladiators he escaped, and defeated a small force sent after them.

During the next two years 70,000 slaves joined his ranks. They defeated the Roman army many times before finally losing to them in 71 BCE. Spartacus's body was never found.

Some gladiators were women

Women gladiators, called gladiatrixes, appeared in the arena from about 60 AD. A marble carving from **Halicarnassus** shows two female gladiators named 'Amazon' and 'Achillia'. Their fight ended in a draw. Gladiatrixes might also have hunted boar and fought from chariots.

Glossary

amphitheatre An open building with tiers of seats around a central space.

Commodus Roman Emperor from 180 to 192 AD.

editor The controller of a gladiator fight, who decided the victor and the outcome.

elope Run away secretly in order to marry.

emperor The ruler of an empire, in this case the Roman Empire.

Halicarnassus An ancient Greek city in modern-day Turkey that became part of the Roman Empire.

Julius Caesar (100 to 45 BCE) A famous general and ruler of Rome. He was the first to invade Britain in 55 BCE and had conquered Gaul by 51 BCE.

Mark Antony (83 to 30 BCE) A Roman politician and general who was a loyal friend of Julius Caesar.

Roman Empire (27 BCE to 476 AD) A huge territory governed by Rome that extended from Britain to Egypt and from Spain and Portugal to Syria.

senator A member of a group of citizens who governed Rome.

Thracian A group of tribes living in Central and Southeastern Europe, west of the Black Sea.

Tiberius Roman Emperor from 14 to 37 AD.

Index